A BOOK FOR MY GRANDCHILD

WELLERAN POLTARNEES

LAUGHING ELEPHANT

MMVII

ISBN13 978-1-59583-185-9
ISBN 1-59583-185-1

LAUGHING ELEPHANT BOOKS
3645 INTERLAKE AVENUE NORTH   SEATTLE, WA 98103

WWW.LAUGHINGELEPHANT.COM

My darling Grandchild -
here are some
of my wishes
for a long
and
wonderful life:

A flight of birds to remind you,
whenever you look up at them,
of the joy of freedom

Trees in springtime - as proof of the beauty and persistence of life

Many windows - offering the
perpetual joy of looking out
at our wonderful world

Many mirrors - so that you may better know yourself

Clouds - for their peacefulness, their lightness

Works of art - which inspire through beauty, transform our vision and spur us to create

Glowing fireplaces - a token of the warmth of home

Many books - for they are doors to other lives and great adventures

Cats - for their
grace and self-possession

And dogs - for their
faithfulness and sense of fun

And afternoon cups of tea - a symbol of quiet pleasures

HONOR C APPLETON

21

Kites - to remind
you to reach even higher

Rainbows - which
offer us everlasting hope

And hearts -
to remind you of my love.

PICTURE CREDITS